Creating Ephemeral Woodland Art for a Deeper Nature Connection
By Brenda Spitzer

Foreword by M. Amos Clifford

Copyright ©2020 by Brenda Spitzer

All rights reserved. No part of this publication may be reproduced or transmitted in any form or by any means, electronic or mechanical, including photocopying, recording, or by any information storage and retrieval system without permission in writing from Brenda Spitzer.
Reviewers may quote brief passages.

Creating Ephemeral Woodland Art
for a Deeper Nature Connection
By Brenda Spitzer

Library of Congress Control Number:
Print ISBN: 978-0-578-63584-2

Publisher: Association of Nature and Forest Therapy
Phone: +1 707 385 1563
Website: natureandforesttherapy.org

Cover Design and Book Design: Michele Lott Design
Photography credits: Lara Benefield, Brenda Spitzer
and Chloe Exiner (back cover)

*To my parents, Edward and Kathleen, who introduced me
to the beauty of the natural world.*

*To my husband, Don, whose love, support and encouragement have
made my dreams a possibility.*

*To my children, Brian, Rebecca and Brad, who taught me
how to treasure each moment.*

*To my grandchildren, Chloe, Autumn, Leona and Westley and to my
great granddaughter, Amber who have guided me on many adventures
and helped me notice the tiny, precious things.*

Foreword
by M. Amos Clifford

Imagination is the soul's bridge into the wild knowing of our deepest Self. In Forest Therapy we speak of the imaginal function, by which we mean the uncountable myriad of ways that the forest speaks to us by making impressions on our imagination. This is not imagination as fantasy, but an active imagination that is also a way of sensing, of knowing. The challenge for most of us is how to become receptive to what the forest is saying. It speaks not in words, but in impulses and feelings that come forth most clearly when they are embodied. Over-thinking kills these imaginal offerings.

We learn how to navigate the imaginal world as a kind of partnership, in which we allow our playfulness to guide our connections with what the forest offers. The forest constantly invites us to express our emergent relationship with it; we can talk out loud to trees and stones, sing to creeks and birds, move, dance, sit, wander, get lost, get found, and so on. All are powerful, all are good. But spontaneous creation of ephemeral works of art is where it all comes together. That's what this book is about.

Brenda Spitzer, whom I've known for several years, is one of the wisest forest therapy guides I have encountered. This book offers a sample of the methods she uses. They are simple, fun, and some people will experience them as profound. Each invitation is simultaneously a calling in and a letting, an exploration of new territory and a coming home. This is a book that shows us how to practice one of the most important aspects of forest therapy. I am grateful to Brenda for sharing her wisdom.

Introduction

Perhaps you enjoy being outside, wandering in the natural environment and making surprising discoveries along the way.

You may have the opportunity to spend time in nature being guided by the children in your life as they make discoveries.

Do you believe in the value of slowing down, living in the moment, and connecting with nature? I would like to invite you to deepen your connection with the natural world by exploring and creating ephemeral art.

Some of my earliest memories in nature involve digging in the dirt outside of my front door. My childhood home was on a hill in Cleveland, Ohio a few miles from Lake Erie. When I played in the dirt, I often found natural treasures like small seashells and smooth, white pebbles that my friends and I called lucky stones. My treasure hunt continued when I visited the home of my grandparents, about 50 miles east of Cleveland. My cousins and I loved to dig in my grandmother's garden. We were told that we might find Native American arrowheads buried there. I remember my cousins discovering pointed objects that we were certain had to be the treasured arrowheads. My favorite found treasure, however, was a small, flat rock that was shaped like a bison. It made me wonder if it had once been an amulet or perhaps someone had carved it as a toy for a child.

Along with my childhood treasure hunting memories, I can recall the summer breeze that would carry the scent of newly mown pastures, the joy of climbing an apple tree in my grandparents yard, the crispy taste of a freshly picked apple, the sound of distant freight trains, and the sight of the bright green duckweed on a nearby pond. Today, these childhood memories come back to me as I wander in nature, especially on sunny days when a gentle breeze is blowing. These memories inspire me to keep noticing and exploring.

Several years ago, I became a trail patrol volunteer at The Morton Arboretum. This new role gave me an opportunity, and a valid reason, to be out on the trails for extended periods of time. After my shifts, I noticed that I felt happier, relaxed and more in tune

with the world around me. I first heard the term 'forest therapy', about five years ago, in a Sustainable Landscape class that I was taking at a local community college. As I listened to our instructor describe the practice of forest therapy and the benefits that it provided, I realized that I had been experiencing similar benefits while on trail patrol.

When I learned that The Morton Arboretum was offering a Forest Therapy Guide Training Workshop, I immediately signed up! I attended this workshop in 2015 and was certified in 2016. I have now had the opportunity to guide more than 100 walks for over 1,000 participants. It has been an honor to guide participants to slow down, tune into their senses, connect with nature, and take a break from the stresses of daily life.

A favorite invitation on each walk is 'Sit Spot'. During this invitation I invite participants to find a special spot in nature to which they feel drawn. At that spot they can sit or wander and use all of their senses to get to know the area and honor their sense of place. I invite them to also notice the moment in which they find themselves. If they wish, they gather natural materials and arrange them to create ephemeral art.

Spending time in nature and noticing details of the environment has inspired artists throughout the centuries. Nature also provides a variety of materials that can be used to create ephemeral art throughout the year. Such art is meant to be fluid and temporary. With exposure to natural elements, like wind, rain and snow, this art is meant to return to the earth.

Chapter 1
Process for Creating Ephemeral Art in Nature

The process of creating ephemeral art can be thought of as a ritual of some simple procedures.

Photo courtesy of Lara Benefield

First, allow yourself the space and time to wander in a natural environment to find a spot to which you feel drawn. Spend some time there getting to know this spot by connecting to it using all of your senses.

What sounds are you hearing?
What textures can you feel?
What fragrances are apparent?
Do you have a special feeling or heart sense about this place?
Are you comfortable here?

If so, then settle in to this spot where you can feel free to create.

In his book, 'Morning Altars', Day Schildkret states, "Bring your full, loving, enormous attention to a place as a gift of love. It is how to show respect and care. It is how you learn where you are. It is how you can learn the language of a place."

Next, gather natural materials, in and around your spot. Notice the shapes, colors, lines, textures and smells of materials as you gather them. Think of this step as a treasure hunt!

The senses, being the explorers of the world,
open the way to knowledge. –Maria Montessori

Once you have gathered materials, clear an area at your spot where you can create your art. After clearing the area, spend some time honoring and appreciating its emptiness before you begin to create something new there.

When we approach things with reverence, great things decide to approach us. –John O'Donohue

Next, play with your gathered materials in your spot. Let your intuition guide you. As you play with your materials, you may discover new ways to arrange them. Let your materials express themselves. Let go of any expectations that you may have about how a final product should look. This is a process of discovery that will unfold as you play. Let your heart guide your hands to arrange the many distinct pieces that you gathered. Stay in the process of play until you feel that your arrangement of materials is complete. You will then have created an ephemeral work of art, something new that has never been in that spot before.

The creation of something new is not accomplished by intellect, but by the play instinct acting from inner necessity. The creative mind plays with the objects it loves. –Carl Jung

Once your artwork is complete, dedicate it to someone or something, if you wish. Think about the intentions you had as you created your art. Intentions can be expressed verbally or they can be written in a journal.

Photo courtesy of Lara Benefield

Next, share your artwork and your intentions with others, if you wish. This can be done through photographs or in real time.

Once you have dedicated and shared your artwork, recognize its impermanence. Ephemeral art is meant to be fluid and temporary. Over time and through exposure to the seasons and the weathering effect of natural elements, such art is meant to return to the earth.

Photo courtesy of Lara Benefield

Art, nature, and ritual have always offered a light in dark places. They can tether us to presence, purpose, and beauty during unpredictable times. —Day Schildkret, "Morning Altars"

Chapter 2
Invitations

Invitations are suggestions for ways that you can approach each project. They are not assignments. There is no right or wrong way to go about creating your own art. The photos in this chapter are simply examples of how others have approached the process. Use your intuition to create your art and make each invitation your own.

Artwork by Ann Mitzkus-Chen

Make a Mandala

Gather some natural materials in and around in your spot. Feel free to wander from your spot to gather more materials. Start with a central object. Arrange the materials that you have gathered, into concentric circles around the central object. Your design does not necessarily have to be round.

The Artistry of the Forest
Wander and Observe the 'Artistry of the Forest'. Let this artistry inspire you to create your art.

Make a Magic Carpet or Quilt

Explore and collect longer branches to form a frame, and shorter branches to subdivide the framed shape into sections. Collect natural materials to place in the sections to fill the frame with patterns, much like a quilt or magic carpet. This project can be done individually or with a partner.

Artwork by Lara Benefield and Brenda Spitzer
Photo courtesy of Lara Benefield

Build a Home in Nature
Use natural materials to construct a home for yourself or a smaller home for an animal or, perhaps, a fairy.

Make a Gift for the Forest
Wander and gather natural materials to bring to your spot.
Arrange these materials to make a gift to express your appreciation to the forest.

Gratitude Altar

Settle into your spot. Notice the details around you, the textures, smells, light, patterns and sounds. Think of something for which you feel grateful. For example, it can be a person, place or event. Look around your spot and gather some natural materials. Use these materials to create some nature art that can be a tribute to that for which you are feeling gratitude.

Artwork by Chloe Exiner

Balancing Stones

Wander and gather stones with which to build a rock tower. Use your senses, including touch, hearing, sight, and heart sense as you stack and balance the stones. Try to stack and balance the stones with your eyes open then closed. Think about balance in your life as you work. Some variations would be stacking or arranging stones and twigs, or balancing stones on a fallen log or in a tree crevice

Museum

Collect natural treasures that you find as you explore an area. Bring them back to your spot and display them, as though they are in a museum. For example, your treasures could be arranged on top of rocks, in tree crevices, along fallen logs, or in a defined space on the ground. If you are near an ocean or lake where the tide goes in and out, it is fun to collect treasures at low tide.

Wabi-sabi Tribute
In Japan there is a cultural concept known as 'Wabi-sabi'. This concept encourages appreciation of things that are imperfect, aged, worn, in decay or incomplete. The following is an invitation that can be used to embrace this concept. For this invitation, walk along the trail and notice elements of nature that appear imperfect, worn, aged or incomplete. If you feel drawn to an element, move toward it and spend some time with it. Notice details such as texture, light patterns, color, movement, fragrance and sound. Also notice how the details of this element resonate within you. Gather materials and create a tribute to honor the Wabi-sabi that you have noticed.

Make a Forest Friend

Explore the area and gather natural materials that you can use to create a Forest Friend.

Twig Frame

For this project you will need some twigs, dried grasses, jute or raffia. Find 4 twigs of the same length, or use pruners to cut them to the same size. Place the twigs, with their ends intersecting, to form a square or rectangle. Use jute or raffia to bind the corners to hold the frame together. If you wish, suspend the frame from a tree branch to frame a specific view. Natural items that you collect can also be attached or suspended within the frame.

Twig Weaving

For this project you will need a forked branch, dried grasses, jute or raffia. Wrap and weave dried grasses, jute or raffia around and through the forks of the branch, several times. Collect natural materials such as leaves, flowers, grasses or feathers and work them into the woven strands between the forks.

Journey Sticks

For this project you will need a sturdy branch that is long enough to be used as a walking stick, dried grasses, jute and/or raffia and natural items that you collect. As you walk along, notice and collect items that attract you. Beginning at the top of the stick and working your way down, attach your found items to the stick using dried grasses, jute and/or raffia. Once you return from your journey, tell someone about your travels by describing the items along your stick, where you found them and what attracted you to them.

Leaf Flags

Thread colorful, fallen leaves on thin branches. Position one end of each branch in the ground in a patch of sunlight to see the colors glow!

Messy projects
Let us embrace the qualities of water and mud!

Leaf Rainbow

Wander and collect colorful leaves. Find a curvy or interesting branch on a tree. Use mud to attach stems of leaves to back of branch so that leaves stand upright, forming a colorful rainbow. A sunny day really brings out the colors of the leaves.

Photo courtesy of Lara Benefield

Texture Exploration Group Sculpture

Members of the group explore the environment noticing the textures of natural items that they encounter along the way. They notice how the texture feels as they touch it and also how the texture of that item resonates within them. Everyone collects one textural, natural item of their choice and brings it back to a predetermined central meeting spot. Each group member then places their item in the center of the meeting spot, one at a time, to create a group sculpture.

Artwork by Retta and John Hennessy, Jackie Reeves and Rebecca Exiner

Tree Mud Faces
Gather some mud from the creek bank. Find a tree to which you are attracted. Use mud to give the tree a face, by forming features such as eyes, eyebrows, nose, mouth, and ears. Use moss, berries, stones and other natural materials to further embellish the face!

Let's... Yes! Let's!
I would like to acknowledge Ben Page and Amos Clifford for this playful partner invitation!

Think back to a time in childhood when you had fun just playing with a friend. Find a partner and meander together along the trails. Partner #1 suggests an activity and says "Let's…. (for example, Let's pick up sticks!)"
Partner #2 responds, "Yes! Let's!"
Wander along together engaging in this activity until Partner #2 makes a suggestion, such as, "Let's build something with our sticks!"
Partner #1 responds, "Yes, let's!"

Continue enjoying this invitation for as long as you wish.

Movement Invitations

Move With Nature: Wander to find a spot to which you feel drawn. Spend some time there noticing movement and activity in the environment. You may notice active motion, like grasses or tree branches moving with the wind.

Or perhaps you will notice non-visual motion that you sense within a natural element, such as shapes, lines, and the natural motion of growth. Use your whole body to imitate this natural motion. Moving this way can feel like a dance with nature.

As you move, notice if you sense a shift in your emotional state. Repeat this process with another motion in the environment for as long as you would like. You can also use your sketchbook to draw, or replicate a movement on a page.

If you wish, you can also express yourself by singing, writing poetry or playing a musical instrument.

Tread a Pattern in the Snow
Find a fresh field of snow. Tread a pattern into the snow as you walk.

Quotes from participants
of my Ephemeral Woodland Art classes:

"I loved this way of creating instead of coming up with a pre-formed plan like I do in my regular day-to-day decision making. This process allowed me to be in the moment and present with the space around me."

Artwork by Retta Hennessy

"My hands were the leader in my process. My hands were attracted to specific natural materials, perhaps because my senses were working with my hands. I wanted to feel the mud and use it to bind my materials together. My hands seemed to operate intuitively. I don't have artistic training or formal experience, but my hands seemed comfortable. This is a great process because it is accessible for everyone."

Artwork by Jackie Reeves

"My heart and emotions felt still and open. I was open to seeing what creations unfolded before me, and then, feeling what connections those creations made with my internal world."

*"After the invitation to create a 'Forest Friend'–
I had no idea what to do. I had to walk around for a while to
find something that would work, and then all of a sudden my friend,
'Henry' appeared! It was a gratifying experience going from having no
idea what to do, to actually creating art."*

Artwork by Rebecca Exiner

Useful supplies to take along

Jute or raffia

Set of colored markers, pencils or crayons

Sketchbook/journal

Pen or pencil

Foraging bags or baskets

A few smaller bags for gathering delicate things

Small broom

Camp stool or mat for sitting

Insect repellant and sunscreen

Water to drink and snack

Waterproof shoes

Clothing that you do not mind getting dirty

Pruning shears

Conclusion

Creating art provides a way for us to visually express the connection of our outer natural world to our inner world. It allows us to honor our sense of place in a special moment in time. By finding our place and collecting the materials that nature provides we can use our hearts, minds, and hands together to express our inner feelings as we create a tribute to our outer world.

Photo courtesy of Lara Benefield

Resources and Recommended Reading

Melanie Choukas-Bradley
The Joy of Forest Bathing: Reconnect With Wild Places and Rejuvenate Your Life
New York: Rock Point an imprint of Quarto Publishing Group, 2018

M. Amos Clifford
Your Guide to Forest Bathing: Experience the Healing Power of Nature
Newburyport, MA: Conari, 2018

Marc Pouyet
Natural, Simple Land Art Through the Seasons
London: Frances Lincoln, Ltd., 2009

Day Schildkret
Morning Altars: A Seven Step Practice to Nourish Your Spirit Through Nature, Art, and Ritual
New York: The Countryman Press,
A Division of W.W. Norton & Company, Inc., 2018

Theresa Sweeney, Ph.D.
Eco-Art Therapy, Creative Activities That Let the Earth Teach
ecoart-therapy.org, 2013

Brenda Spitzer grew up in Northeast Ohio. She and her husband, Donald, currently live in Wheaton, Illinois. They have three grown children and four grandchildren and one great grandchild. Brenda became a Certified Forest Therapy Guide for The Association of Nature and Forest Therapy Guides and Programs in 2015. She also has a Bachelor of Arts in Art from Northern Illinois University and Certificates in Botanical Art and Illustration and Natural History from The Morton Arboretum. She introduced the "Nature Rx: Forest Therapy Walk" program at The Morton Arboretum in 2016, and has been guiding forest therapy walks there for the past 4 years. She often incorporates creating ephemeral art into her forest therapy walks. She also guides walks for The Western Dupage Special Recreation Association. She enjoys spending time exploring natural areas with her five grandchildren. As they explore, she always allows them to be the guide.

Photo courtesy of Lara Benefield

Journaling

Made in the USA
Monee, IL
26 March 2021